Sign up for our newsletter to hear
about new and upcoming releases.

www.ylva-publishing.com

Books in the

Writers' Guide Series

Goal Setting for Writers
How to set and achieve your writing goals, write a book, and become a successful author

Time Management for Writers
How to write faster, find the time to write your book, and be a more prolific writer

Show, Don't Tell
How to write vivid descriptions, handle backstory, and describe your characters' emotions

Point of View
How to use the different POV types, avoid head-hopping, and choose the best point of view for your book

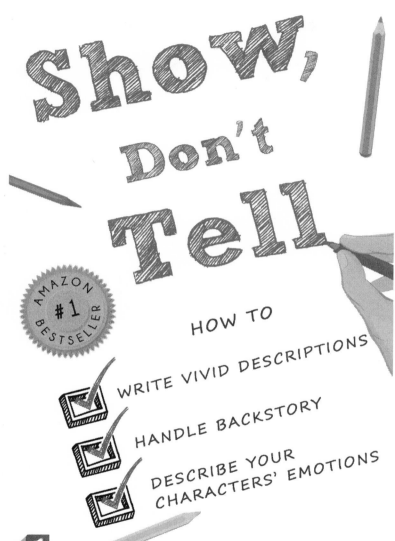

Show, Don't Tell

AMAZON #1 BESTSELLER

HOW TO

☑ WRITE VIVID DESCRIPTIONS

☑ HANDLE BACKSTORY

☑ DESCRIBE YOUR CHARACTERS' EMOTIONS

Ylva

SANDRA GERTH

Table of Contents

About Sandra Gerth

Other books from Ylva Publishing

1. Introduction —
What this book will teach you

"Show, don't tell" is probably the single piece of writing advice that beginning writers hear most often from editors and writing coaches. Authors who master this important technique take their writing to the next level and captivate their readers with powerful scenes that keep them turning pages even though it's two in the morning and they have to work the next day.

But many writers struggle to understand this principle or have difficulty applying it to their own work. Even authors who have already published several books often don't grasp the finer nuances of *showing* vs. *telling*.

I know because I was one of them. When I had a few books under my belt, I thought I knew what *showing* meant. But then I realized that I had only just scratched the surface. With every novel I wrote and every book about writing I read, I deepened my understanding and discovered more layers to *show, don't tell*. As an editor and a mentor, I try to teach my writers what I learned about *showing* and *telling*. Since there are only so many writers I can mentor and only so many manuscripts I can edit, I decided to write a book about *show, don't tell* so I can help more writers of all skill levels understand this powerful principle and apply it to their work.

Whether you're a novice writer working on your first story or an established author who has already learned the basics of *showing* and *telling*, this book will help you to:

- grasp the difference between *showing* and *telling*;
- understand why showing is such a powerful tool;
- spot *telling* in your own manuscript;
- fix bland passages and turn them into compelling scenes;
- keep from telling what you have already shown;
- avoid the three danger areas of telling;
- describe your characters and your setting in interesting ways;
- put powerful emotions into your writing;
- incorporate backstory into your novel without resorting to *telling*;
- recognize *telling* in dialogue;
- avoid *overshowing* and swamping your readers with too many details;
- learn when telling is actually a good thing;
- immerse your readers into your story and keep them captivated from beginning to end.

HOW TO GET THE MOST OUT OF THIS BOOK

The only way to improve your writing is by writing, so this book includes not only concrete examples but also exercises so you can practice what you're learning—using your own work in progress, if you want.

I suggest that you print out the first chapter of your manuscript. Get a notebook or several sheets of paper and a pen and some highlighters. While you're reading this book, stop after every chapter and do the exercises. Most of them will have you work on your manuscript, so by the time you finish this book, you'll have a first chapter that is full of good writing that shows instead of tells. Then you can use the techniques you learned on the rest of your manuscript too.

If you don't yet want to practice on your own manuscript—or you don't have a completed first draft yet—there are also twenty exercises in chapter 13 that will help you practice your showing skills.

By the way, a few of the examples I use throughout this book are from my own novels, written under my pen name, Jae (jae-fiction. com). I do that strictly for legal reasons, to make sure I'm not violating anyone's copyright. A few of the examples are based on manuscripts I edited, rewritten to protect the innocent.

Happy reading and writing!
Sandra Gerth

2. Definition —
What show, don't tell means

At some point in their writing career, all writers get the advice to *show*, not *tell*.

"Show us that she's a spoiled little girl; don't tell us!"

"Show us that he lives in a run-down apartment building; don't tell us!"

"Show us that she's angry at her father; don't tell us!"

While that's certainly good advice, many writing coaches, instructors, and editors fail to explain what it means.

So, let's start by defining showing and telling.

• **Telling** means that you—the author—give your readers conclusions and interpretations; you tell them what to think instead of letting them think for themselves.
Showing means that you provide your readers with enough concrete, vivid details so that they can draw their own conclusions.

• **Telling** is like giving readers a secondhand report afterward.
Showing lets readers experience the events firsthand, through the five senses of the character.

- **Telling** is like reading about an accident in the newspaper the day after it happened.
  Showing is like witnessing the accident the moment it happens, hearing the screech of the metal and the screams of the injured.

- **Telling** summarizes events that happened in the past or gives general statements that don't happen at any specific time.
  Showing lets readers witness events in real time, in actual scenes with action and dialogue. We stay in the present, firmly rooted in the POV character's experience.

- **Telling** is abstract.
  Showing creates a concrete, specific picture in the reader's mind.

- **Telling** gives you facts.
  Showing evokes emotions.

- **Telling** is also called narrative summary.
  Showing is dramatization.

- **Telling** distances readers from the events in the story and from the characters and makes them passive recipients of information.
  Showing involves readers in the story and makes them active participants.

AN EXAMPLE

Okay, now that I've *told* you what the difference is, let me *show* you by giving you an example:

```
Tina was angry.
```

This is telling. The author is handing readers a conclusion.

```
Tina slammed the door shut and stormed into the
kitchen. "What the hell were you thinking?"
```

This is showing. It gives the readers the concrete actions and the character's dialogue so that they can come to the conclusion that Tina is angry without the author stating it flat-out.

EXERCISE #1:

- Get out a notebook or a sheet of paper and try your hand at the "Tina was angry" sentence. How would you show your readers that Tina is angry without stating her emotions? Use actions, body language, and dialogue to show her anger.

3. The importance of showing — Why showing is usually better than telling

Telling isn't always bad. As we'll see in a later chapter, it definitely has its uses, but most of the time, you want to show.

Why?

Think about why we read novels. Unlike readers of nonfiction, fiction readers don't read to get information. They read to be entertained and to escape into another world.

The same is true for people who want to see a movie (not a documentary). Now imagine you are sitting in a movie theater, waiting for the movie to start, and instead, the person sitting next to you tells you all the interesting parts. I bet you wouldn't be happy, right? You didn't want to be told about the movie; you wanted to watch the movie for yourself and get so caught up in it that you forget everything else for a while. Well, readers are the same. They want to experience the story for themselves and share the characters' struggles—and that can be achieved only with showing, not telling.

Telling doesn't evoke images in the reader's mind. It interprets the information for the reader and robs them of the opportunity to think and discover the story world for themselves.

Showing keeps readers actively engaged because they need to think about what they're reading and interpret what's going on rather than passively being presented with conclusions. That's what draws them in and keeps them turning the pages because they're actively asking questions and read on, curious to find out the answers.

So to fully immerse your readers into your story and make them experience the events along with the protagonist, you need to master the skill of showing.

4. Nine red flags for telling — How to tell when you're telling

Now you know what telling is. But despite that knowledge, it can still be difficult to recognize when those telling instances have somehow crept into your own manuscript. Here are some red flags that indicate telling.

To spot telling, read every sentence you wrote carefully. Keep an eye out for places where you find yourself using one of these red flags for telling.

1) Conclusions

If you give your readers conclusions, you are telling. To show, provide them with enough "evidence" so they can come to the conclusions themselves.

Example:

Telling: It was obvious that he was trying to pick a fight.

As you can see, that's a conclusion. Think about how you could *show* your readers what it was that made it so obvious that he was trying to pick a fight.

Showing: "What did you just say?" Snarling, he stepped forward, right into John's space.

Showing gives us a description of action, body language, facial expressions, and dialogue so that we can conclude that he's trying to pick a fight without the author outright telling us so.

2) Abstract language

If you are using abstract, vague language, you are telling. Take a look at each of your sentences. Can you visualize what's happening? Could you film it? Or maybe, for the people who are familiar with *Star Trek*, a better question would be: could you experience it on a holodeck, since scent, taste, feel, and temperature can't be captured on film. If you can't experience it, you are telling.

Example:

Telling: She checked the man's vital status.

What exactly does "vital status" mean in this context? And what did she do to check it? We're not getting a mental image from this vague description.

Showing: She bent and placed two fingers on his neck. A faint pulse throbbed beneath her fingertips.

3) Summaries

If you sum up what happened, you're telling. Sometimes, I come across a manuscript that reads like a synopsis and that sums up everything that is happening instead of showing it in actual scenes. That's fine if you are actually writing a synopsis, but not for your novel.

Readers don't just want to get a general idea of what happened; they want to see specific details.

Example:

Telling: I found the body in the back of a tarp-covered truck.

If this is a mystery novel or a scene of high emotion in which the protagonist finds a dead body, readers want to see that suspenseful moment, but *found the body* doesn't create an image in the reader's mind.

Showing: I climbed onto the back of the truck and peeled back the tarp. A sickeningly sweet stench made me stumble back. Sightless eyes stared back at me. I pressed a hand to my mouth, smothering a scream.

If you're not sure if you are showing detailed actions or summing them up, try to act out what your characters are doing. If you can't, you're telling. As you might have noticed, the previous example also makes good use of the senses, not just sight but also smell and sound (if you count the smothered scream).

Example:

Telling: The dog attacked. She tried to defend herself.

What exactly did the dog do? Jump? Bite? Growl? And how exactly did she defend herself? Kick the dog? Hide?

Showing: The dog leaped, canines bared. She threw up her arm to protect her throat.

4) Backstory

If you report things that happened in the past, before this very moment, you are telling. For important scenes, show your readers what is happening as it's happening, in real time, instead of summing up what happened a few minutes ago. A good indicator for when you might be reporting things that happened in the past is if you find yourself using the past perfect (see the *had tested* in the example below). To find places where you might have used too much backstory, type *had* into the search box of your writing software and look for paragraphs with verbs in their past perfect form. See if you can rewrite and show us the scene in simple past tense.

Example:

Telling: I had tested the car to see if it would start. It didn't.

Showing: I turned the key in the ignition. A click-click-click-click noise drifted up from the engine. I smashed my fist into the steering wheel. "Dammit!"

5) Adverbs

If you find yourself using an adverb, you are usually telling. Whenever possible, cut the adverbs. Sometimes, the sentence is just fine without it; other times, you might want to rewrite the sentence and replace the weak verb/adverb combination with a stronger verb that makes the adverb unnecessary. Of course, you shouldn't cut all adverbs from your writing, but use them sparingly.

Example 1:

Telling: The dog tucked its tail between its legs and whined anxiously.

Showing: The dog tucked its tail between its legs and whined.

The posture and whining *shows* the dog's anxiety, so there's no need to add the adverb.

Example 2:

Telling: "Don't lie to me," she shouted angrily.
Showing: "Don't lie to me, dammit." She slammed her palm on the table.

Her word choice and her action show that she's angry, without stating the emotion.

Example 3:

Telling: Tina slowly walked down the street.
Showing: Tina strolled down the street.

The adverb (slowly) tells your readers how Tina walks; the strolled shows it.

6) Adjectives

Like adverbs, adjectives can also be telling, especially if they are abstract adjectives such as *interesting* or *beautiful*.

Example:

Telling: I was afraid.
Showing: Oh God, oh God, oh God. My knees felt like squishy sponges as I fled down the stairs.

7) Linking verbs

Adjectives can often be found in combination with linking verbs. Linking verbs are verbs that connect a subject with an adjective or noun. Examples are *was/were*, *is/are*, *felt*, *appeared*, *seemed*, *looked*. The problem with them is that they are weak, static verbs that don't show us an action. Replace most of them with more active verbs.

Examples (with the linking verbs set off in italics):

Telling: It *was* cold.
Showing: She breathed into her hands to warm her numb fingers.

Telling: Tina *felt* tired.
Showing: She rubbed her eyes.

Telling: Tina *seemed* impressed.
Showing: Tina's eyes widened, and her lips formed a silent, "Wow!"

Telling: Tina *looked* as if she was going to cry.
Showing: Tina's bottom lip started to quiver.

8) Emotion words

When you're naming emotions, you are telling. Keep an eye out for adjectives such as "surprised" and "angry" and nouns such as "amazement" and "confusion." You might even start a list of the emotion words you use most often, to make sure you can catch them during the revisions.

Instead of naming emotions, use actions, thoughts, visceral reactions, and body language to show what your characters are feeling. More on that in the chapter on showing emotions.

Example:

Telling: When John left, Betty and Tina were relieved.

Showing: When the door closed behind John, Betty wiped her brow and Tina exhaled the breath she'd been holding.

At times, naming an emotion can work, though, if you make the emotion word the sentence's subject and pair it with a strong verb. But use this technique sparingly, or it will start to jump out at the reader.

Example :

Fear clawed at her like a wild animal.

9) Filters

Filter words are verbs that describe the character perceiving or thinking something, for example, *saw*, *smelled*, *heard*, *felt*, *watched*, *noticed*, *realized*, *wondered*, and *knew*. The problem is that filter words tell your readers what the character perceives or thinks instead of letting them experience it directly. Readers are forced to watch the character from the outside instead of being in her head, experiencing things along with her. So, cut out the "she realized" and "he saw" and make the sentence just about the thing she realized or the sound he heard.

Examples:

Telling: Tina heard Betty suck in a breath.
Showing: Betty sucked in a breath.

Telling: `Tina realized she had lost her keys.`
Showing: `Tina patted her pockets. Nothing.` *Oh shit. Where were her keys?*

Here, we—the readers—get to witness the realization without the author telling us she had a realization.

REVISION TIP

For some of these red flags, you can use the search feature of your writing software to find and replace them.

- To find adverbs, type *ly* into the search box, or if you know which adverbs you overuse, e.g., *quickly*, *softly*, *gently*, do a search for them.
- You can also search for filter words such as *wondered*, *realized*, or *heard*.
- For emotion words, type in the noun, adjective, and adverb form of emotions such as *anger*, *angry*, and *angrily*.
- Also search for linking verbs such as *felt*, *was*, or *seemed*.

Revise each of them and turn *telling* into *showing*, using the tips and examples above to guide you.

EXERCISE #2:

- Print out the first scene of your work in progress and read it line by line. Can you detect any of the red flags for telling? Can you picture everything you have described, or have you used abstract words, for example?

- If you are working on your computer or laptop, use the find feature to search for red flags such as adverbs, emotion words, and filters, as described above. If you use pen and paper, try to spot any adverbs, adjectives, filters, or emotion words in the scene.

- Have you used past perfect, which can be a red flag for telling readers about things that happened in the past?

- Highlight all instances of telling that you can find in your first scene.

5. The art of showing —
How to turn telling into showing

So now that you know how to spot telling, what showing is, and why you should do it, let's take a look at *how* to show. Here are the nine top tips on how to show:

1) Use the five senses

Showing means letting your readers experience your story world along with the point of view character. Try to engage all of your readers' senses, not just sight. In every scene, put yourself in your POV character's shoes and describe what he can see, hear, smell, taste, and sense.

Example:

> I stuck my nose out of the car's open window and breathed in the fresh pine scent. The cold air made my cheeks burn and my eyes tear.

2) Use strong, dynamic verbs

Make your writing come to life by using strong, active verbs, not verbs that are weak and static. For example, instead of saying *she walked*, use *she strutted*, *she strode*, *she trudged*, or *she tiptoed* to show us exactly how she moves. Keep on the lookout for weak verbs—usually all forms of *to be* (including the overused *there was* and *there were*) and *to have*—and replace them with verbs that paint a clearer picture in the reader's mind.

Example:

Telling: The man was thin and wore a coat that was too big for him.

Showing: His coat hung around his frame.

Verbs that can also weaken your writing are *started to* and *began to*.

Example:

Weak verb: The woman started to shake.

Without the weak verb: The woman shook.

Or maybe even better: Fine tremors rushed through the woman's body.

Be careful not to overdo it, though. At times, you just want your characters to walk across a room, without drawing attention to it, instead of strutting, trudging, or tiptoeing. If the action is not that important, using a weaker verb is fine. But if you want to build suspense and tension, use the stronger verb to show what your character is feeling while she walks.

3) Use concrete nouns

Try to be as specific as possible rather than using generic terms. That's not just true for verbs, but for nouns too. Use concrete nouns that create the image you want in readers' minds. Instead of having your characters eat breakfast, let your readers know that they're having eggs and bacon. Instead of telling readers that your protagonist has a dog, show them a drooling Great Dane.

Example:

Telling: `Tina lived in a big house.`

Showing: `Tina's steps echoed across the foyer as she entered the mansion.`

4) Break activities into smaller parts

One trick to write in a more concrete way is to break generic activities into smaller parts. Instead of telling us that your protagonist is cleaning, show us that she's vacuuming and frowning at the sock she finds beneath the couch.

Don't overdo it, though. If the activity isn't important, sum it up in a general sweep. But if it reveals something about the character— maybe how fastidious she is—or moves the plot forward, break it down into its parts. If she finds not a sock but drugs beneath her son's bed, it might be worth showing your readers the details instead of just saying *she was cleaning*.

5) Use figurative language

One way to create images in readers' minds and make your writing more vivid is the use of figurative language, especially similes and metaphors. A simile is a figure of speech that compares two things using the words *like* or *as*, e.g., her hair shone like gold. A metaphor compares two things more directly, e.g., the company was a gold mine.

Example:

Telling: `Betty had callused palms.`

Showing: `Betty's palms felt like sandpaper.`

The best metaphors and similes always come from the character's background. For example, a character who would think that Betty's palms felt like sandpaper clearly has experience with sandpaper. Maybe he or she is an artist working with wood or a carpenter. A person who doesn't have that kind of background would use a different comparison.

Be careful not to overdo it, though. If you use too many metaphors and similes, your writing will come across as pretentious and overwritten. Metaphors and similes can also become clichés, so try not to use the first thing that comes to mind.

6) Write in real time

Make sure you write in scenes and let the action unfold in real time. Instead of summing up what happened, let your readers witness the moment-to-moment action. Again, a red flag that indicates that you are no longer writing in real time is the use of past perfect, e.g., *she had gone.*

You don't need to show everything in real time, of course; otherwise, your novel will be full of meaningless actions that will read like filler. As I will discuss in chapter 12, at times, telling can be a great tool to compress the nonessential parts. It's the important scenes—the ones that move the plot forward or reveal something about a character— that you want to show.

7) Use dialogue

One way to show the action in real time is to write dialogue. Dialogue is always showing—at least if you do it right. More about showing and telling in dialogue in a later chapter.

Example:

Telling: `Tina was a flirt.`

Showing: `"Well, hello,"` Tina drawled. `"The view in here just got a lot better."`

8) Use internal monologue

Showing what your POV character is thinking can also help to reveal her emotions without having to name them.

Example:

Telling: `I was relieved when my workday ended.`

Showing: `Finally, the bell rang, announcing the end of my workday.` *`Thank the Lord.`*

9) Focus on actions and reactions

You have probably heard the saying *actions speak louder than words*. Just telling your readers that your character is a mean, bitter woman might not be enough for them to believe it. Showing her kick a puppy will immediately convince your readers that she's mean.

Instead of telling your readers about your characters' personality traits, let them get to know the characters through their actions. Let them see how they act and react to the story events, which will *show* their personality. Telling keeps your characters passive; showing reveals their personality through actions.

Example 1:

Telling: Tina was a loyal friend. She always helped out whenever one of her acquaintances or family members needed her.

This reads more like one of the character sketches I'm doing before I start writing a new novel than something that belongs into a scene. It *tells* the readers what Tina is like instead of *showing* her in action and letting the readers get to know her.

Showing: "Come on." Tina patted her shoulder. "Assembling the furniture won't be that bad. You know what they say about many hands." She picked up the screwdriver.

Example 2:

Telling: Jake had always been a little clumsy.
Showing: When he reached out to pick up the saltshaker, he knocked over his wineglass.

EXERCISE #3:

- Take another look at the first scene of your work in progress. Can you spot a place where you could use the five senses to describe something your character can see, hear, smell, taste, or touch? Draw your readers more firmly into your story world by adding a few lines of vivid sensory description.

EXERCISE #4:

- Are there any weak, static verbs in your first scene? Do you have a lot of *had*'s and *was*'s? Do your characters *walk slowly* instead of *trudging* or do they *walk quickly* instead of *sprinting*, for example? See if you can replace some of the weak verbs with stronger ones

EXERCISE #5:

- Look at your chapter one. Have you stated any personality traits? Look for words such as "Tina was... (a loyal friend)" or "Tina liked...(gossiping)." If you told your readers about your characters, rewrite the scene and try to show those personality traits through actions.

6. Redundancies —
How to avoid telling what you have already shown

Another common mistake I often see in manuscripts I'm editing is passages that show and tell the same thing. Sometimes, writers have beautifully shown something, but instead of moving on, they add a tell, as if to make sure that readers really "got it."

Example:

    Betty glanced down at the hand on her arm, her
    eyes flashing with anger.

The flashing eyes *show* her anger; the "with anger" *tells* us she's angry. Just cut the telling. If you don't quite trust the sentence to reveal the character's emotions without the telling, rewrite the sentence to show more strongly.

Rewrite:

    Betty glanced down at the hand on her arm, her
    eyes flashing.

Or:

    Betty glared at the hand on her arm.

Example 2:

> Betty's brow wrinkled. "I don't know if that's such a good idea." She obviously wasn't convinced.

The wrinkled brow and her words *show* that she's not convinced, so you don't need that last sentence. Try not to tell things you have already shown. Trust your showing skills, and trust your readers to get what you're trying to say just from the showing part.

Rewrite:

> Betty's brow wrinkled. "I don't know if that's such a good idea."

EXERCISE #6:

- Look at your first scene again. Have you told anything that you have already shown? If so, cross out the telling parts and let the showing stand on its own.

7. Danger area 1 —
How to handle backstory

In one of my favorite writing craft books, *Stein on Writing*, Sol Stein lists three danger areas for telling, and I would add one more:

1. Telling readers about events that happened before the story began (Backstory)
2. Telling readers what the characters look like (Character descriptions)
3. Telling readers what the character experience through their senses (Setting descriptions)
4. Telling readers what the characters feel (Emotions)

I will cover each of these danger areas in the next chapters. Let's start with backstory, since I find that this is probably the hardest to get right for most authors.

DEFINITION OF BACKSTORY

Basically, backstory is everything that happened prior to page one of your book, for example, events from your character's childhood or past relationships. Backstory is important because it shapes who your characters are today and how they will react to things that happen in the story.

THE PROBLEM WITH BACKSTORY

So, what's the problem with backstory?

• Backstory, especially if you introduce it too early, **kills suspense**. Start your story in media res—in the middle of things. Throw your readers into the story and let them wonder what led to the character being in this situation. Unanswered questions are a good thing because they'll keep your readers turning the pages to find out the answers. If you give them all the information, there's no need to continue reading and they'll get bored.

• Backstory **isn't story**. Your readers want to find out what happens in the present instead of hearing about things that are long over.

• Backstory **is often dumped on readers much too soon**. I often see manuscripts in which the character sits and thinks about her past in chapter one. The opening pages isn't the best place to reveal a character's backstory because readers haven't become emotionally involved yet. They need to become caught up in the present first before they care about a character's past.

• Backstory **slows down the pacing**. Information about the past stops the forward momentum of the story.

HOW TO REVEAL BACKSTORY

So now that you know what problems backstory can cause, how do you handle it in a way that avoids these issues?

• **Don't be afraid of unanswered questions**. Don't think you need to give readers all the information about why your character is acting in a certain way as soon as we see the action. Delay the answers and create a need within readers so by the time you drop in bits of backstory, they want to know and won't find it boring. Hook your readers by not revealing too much, too soon.

- **Anchor your readers in the present first** and make them care for the characters before revealing backstory. Instead of starting your novel with backstory, open it with an event that happens in the present. Many editors even advise writers to keep backstory out of the first fifty pages of their manuscripts.

- **Don't dump large blocks of backstory on the reader all at once.** If you need to reveal backstory, keep it short. Don't stop the action while you explain your characters' past to readers. Reveal it bit by bit as the story unfolds, just a few sentences here and a few sentences there so that the backstory doesn't stop the forward momentum of the story too much.

- **Reveal only the bits of backstory that are important to the present.** Every piece of backstory you include in your story must matter. If the reader doesn't need the information right now, leave it out—or wait until it becomes necessary. Cut out whatever backstory isn't essential for the scene and then give your manuscript to beta readers. Ask them to comment on anything that confuses them. Those might be the places where you might need to include a bit of backstory.

- **Use the iceberg principle**: While you as the author know every little detail about how your characters grew up, what jobs they had in the past, and what relationships shaped them, readers don't need to know all of that. Most of that should stay hidden beneath the surface while readers see only the tip of the iceberg. They'll be able to sense that there's more, and that's all they need.

- **Turn the backstory into story by bringing the past into the present.** For example, in my novel *Just Physical*, my main character is a stuntwoman who got hurt in a fire stunt in the past. But instead of telling my readers that fact, I show her fear as she has to do a fire stunt in the present.

- **Reveal backstory through dialogue.** If one of the characters finds out information about the other character in a conversation, readers can learn about it along with the character. In order to reveal backstory through dialogue in a realistic way, though, you need one character who doesn't know about the piece of backstory already. Don't create As-you-know-Bob dialogue in which characters talk about things they both already know and have no reason to talk about, just so readers can be brought up to speed.

Example from my novel *Hidden Truths*:

"Call me Phin." He reached for her hand and rested it in the crook of his elbow, then set them off for a stroll along the corrals. "When you call me Phineas, I feel like my father is standin' behind me."

"And that wouldn't be a good thing?"

"No. My father was a real bastard." He blanched. "Um. Pardon my language."

- **Add conflict**: You can add conflict and make it more interesting for readers if you make one character reluctant to reveal information about his or her past, so the other character has to fight for it.

FLASHBACKS

Another way to reveal backstory is through flashbacks—an acted-out scene that shows, not tells something that happened in the past, including actions and dialogue. Flashbacks are a form of *showing*; you write a fully dramatized scene.

The advice most editors give to writers about flashbacks is not to use them, though. Flashbacks jerk the reader out of the flow of the story and stop the book's forward momentum. Often, it would be better to use a few lines of *telling* to avoid using a flashback. You'll find out more about the uses of telling in chapter 12.

If you feel you must include a flashback because there's no other way to reveal a bit of backstory, here's how to handle it:

- **Keep the flashback scene short.** If you interrupt the present story for too long, readers might have problems settling back into it—and might even stop reading altogether.

- **Don't use flashback scenes in the first third of your novel.** Wait until readers are anchored in the present and care about the characters enough to want to see more about their past.

- **Make sure your flashback follows a powerful scene in the present.** If a flashback follows a boring scene, readers have no reason to return to the story.

- **Build in triggers** in the present that make the character remember something from the past.

- **At the start of the flashback, immediately orient your reader in time and place.** Let them know how far they have jumped back in time and where they are.

- Also **use transition words** to let readers know when you're returning to the present (e.g., now).

- **Use verb tense to signal the start and the end of a flashback.** Assuming your novel is told in the past tense, use past perfect (e.g., had seen) two or three times when you enter a flashback and then show us the scene with action and dialogue in simple past tense (e.g., saw). Writing the entire flashback scene in past perfect would be too cumbersome. Once you're about to jump back to the present, use past perfect once or twice and then resume the story in the present with simple past.

Example:

She put her arms behind her head and stared at her old room. It was still the same worn carpet and the same ugly wallpaper as the last time she'd been here fifteen years ago.

Back then, she had been lying on the bed the way she was now, listening to music, when her father had barged into the room.

"Get downstairs," he had said. "Now!"

```
Heart  hammering,  she  rolled  out  of  bed  and
followed him downstairs.
```

```
Her father slammed a letter onto the dining room
table.  "You  applied  to  college  without  telling
me? What about the store?"
```

Then we'd see the entire conflict between father and daughter playing out, written in past tense. Here's an example for a switch back into the here and now of the story:

```
"If that's what you think," her father had said,
his  back  to  her,  "go.  Go  and  never  come  back."
```

```
"I won't," she had shouted.
```

```
Yet  here  she  was,  fifteen  years  later,  staring
at the wall of her childhood bedroom.
```

If the story is written in present tense, the flashback will be in past tense.

- **Don't use italics to set off flashbacks.** Italics are hard to read, so you shouldn't use them for long sections.

- **Avoid flashbacks within flashbacks.** Within your flashback scene, stay in the present and don't have the character think of things that happened even further back in time.

PROLOGUES

You might wonder whether prologues are a good way to include backstory. Prologues are separate scenes that take place months, years, decades, or even centuries before the beginning of the story. They usually reveal something important about the history of the story's world or something that provides context to the story. So, in a way, prologues are similar to flashbacks—and they have their disadvantages too.

Most literary agents and many readers hate prologues. They frustrate readers because they delay the real beginning of the story, but some writers use them anyway because they're convinced that the reader needs to know this piece of information to understand the story.

I'm not saying that you can't write a great prologue that actually works, but most of the time, you're better off without it and you don't really need it. Prologues aren't the best way to reveal backstory. Your readers don't know the protagonist yet, so seeing an event from his or her past won't have any meaning to them at this point. The same is true about a prologue that sets up your story world. Readers don't care much about your world and its history yet.

Instead of dumping information onto the reader in your prologue, start the story where the action begins and then weave in bits of backstory as the plot unfolds and let readers figure it out for themselves.

EXERCISE #7:

- Look through the first chapter of your manuscript. Does it include any backstory—any information about things that happened before the story started? Highlight it. Does the reader really need all this information right now? Tighten the scene by keeping only what is necessary for readers to understand what is happening. Remember that you don't need to answer all questions immediately.
- Can you reveal some of the backstory information in a scene, via dialogue and real-time actions?
- Can some of it be moved to later parts of the story?

8. Danger area 2 —
How to handle descriptions

Remember the danger areas of telling that I mentioned in the previous chapter? Two other danger areas are descriptions of characters and setting.

Description is important because many readers want that movie in their head to start playing, and that can only happen if we give them an idea of what the characters and the setting look like. But how do we do that without resorting to telling?

DESCRIPTIONS OF SETTING

- **Avoid large blocks of description.** In past eras, authors could get away with writing long descriptions of setting, but modern readers don't have the patience to wade through pages and pages of description. They want to get to the action. So instead of huge lumps of information, sprinkle in descriptions bit by bit.

- **The best descriptions are dynamic, not static.** Instead of stopping the story and ignoring the character while you describe the setting, let the character interact with and move through the setting.

Example:

Telling: The living room was furnished with a white leather couch and a coffee table made of glass and chrome.

Was is one of the weak verbs I mentioned.

Showing: Tina rounded the glass-and-chrome contraption that was supposed to be a coffee table and gingerly eased herself down onto the couch, careful not to leave any stains on the white leather.

This description shows us something not just about the setting, but about the character too. Clearly, she doesn't feel comfortable in this setting. Her own living room probably looks a lot different.

- As I mentioned before, **use strong, active verbs**. Even for objects that are static, try to come up with a description that is dynamic and includes some kind of motion.

Example:

Telling: The observatory had a golden dome.
Showing: Sunlight glinted off the observatory's golden dome.

- **Avoid vague nouns and use specific ones** instead. For example, instead of saying that the character parked his car, have him park his Subaru.

- **If you use adjectives, make sure they are descriptive ones**, e.g., sparkling, sky-blue, or star-shaped, not adjectives of opinion, e.g., beautiful, intelligent, or attractive.

- **Use all five senses.** Many writers describe just what the characters see and maybe hear but neglect the other senses. Touch, smell, and taste are more intimate, powerful senses, which evoke emotions and trigger memories in readers, so make sure you use them too.

Example:

```
The scent of salt and sagebrush hung in the
air. I lifted my nose into the ocean breeze and
inhaled deeply.
```

- **Describe only what your POV character would notice given his or her background, personality, and situation.** Different people notice different things. If your character has been in an apartment a thousand times before, she will give it only a passing glance. An interior designer would notice the colors and the arrangement of furniture, while a firefighter would look for the exits. An action scene where the characters are fighting for their lives is not a good place for a description of the beautiful view.

- Give us not just the factual description of the setting but also **show us how the character feels about it**.

Example:

```
She pushed back the tent's flap and wrinkled her
nose. Ugh. The inside of the tent smelled like
sweat, dirty stockings, and damp wool. No way
would she stay in this rat hole.
```

- **Try not to rely on clichés** in your descriptions. Certain phrases such as *smooth as silk* or *as red as a tomato* have become so overused that they bore readers and are no longer memorable.

- Believe it or not, but **dialogue can be used to describe your setting**. Just make sure if feels like something these characters would actually say, not like you—the author—explaining things to the reader.

Here's an example from my novel *Heart Trouble*:

Laleh felt Hope's gaze on her as she looked around. "It's nice," she said, trying to sound enthusiastic. "Very...um, clean and sophisticated."

"It's pretty minimalistic, I know." Hope shrugged. "I'm hardly ever home anyway, and my decorating skills are about as good as my cooking skills."

DESCRIPTIONS OF CHARACTERS

- **Don't describe your character all at once, in one large block of description.** Just like your characters' backstory shouldn't all be revealed in chapter one, you don't need to have a head-to-toe description in the first chapter. Scatter in bits and pieces throughout the first few chapters, without stopping the forward momentum of the story. When the characters first meet, they notice just the most obvious things and then, later, when they move closer, we get the details such as eye color. Also, different people notice different things when they are first meeting someone. That reveals as much about the person you describe as it does about the character observing him or her. Your descriptions are doing double duty, which is always a good thing.

- **Readers don't need to know every little detail** about what the character looks like. Pick the most interesting details and allow the reader's imagination to do the rest.

- The best descriptions are the ones that tell us more than just how the character looks but **reveal something about his or her personality** too.

Example:

```
As they walked to the car next to each other,
Tina slouched, careful not to straighten to her
full height.
```

That shows us that she's tall, and it also reveals that she feels self-conscious about her height.

- If you are **using the words and the figurative language of your POV character** to describe the other characters, your descriptions are doing double duty. They not only show us what the observed character looks like, but they also reveal something about the POV character.

Example from my novel *Something in the Wine*:

```
Golden hair—the color of a fine, mature white
wine—brushed against Annie's slender shoulders.
```

The point of view character, Drew, is a winemaker, and she loves her job, so she uses wine terms to describe Annie's hair color.

- As with setting descriptions, **use strong, dynamic verbs** instead of static ones.

Example:

Telling: She had dark eyes and a friendly smile.
Showing: Her smile crinkled the corners of her dark eyes.

- **Avoid long lists of details**. They're exhausting for readers, and they won't remember all the items in the list anyway.

Example:

Her short, black, figure-hugging skirt revealed her long, slender legs.

I'd strongly suggest cutting a few adjectives. *Short* isn't needed, for example, because if the skirt reveals her legs, we can assume it's short.

- **Use dialogue**: Sometimes, you can even sneak in a bit of character description in your dialogue.

Example:

Tina looked the actress up and down. "You look a lot taller on camera."

EXERCISE #8:

- Look through your first chapter again. Do you have any descriptions of your setting or your characters? Highlight them, and take a look at how long they are. Do you have long blocks of information? If yes, you might want to break them up and weave them into the scene in smaller bits.

- Take a look at the verbs in your descriptions. Could you make your descriptions stronger by replacing some of them with stronger, more dynamic verbs?

- Have you used the five senses in your descriptions? Try to include at least one or two senses other than just sight. What does the place smell like? Are there any sounds? Is your character touching or eating anything that you could describe?

- Do your descriptions reveal a little about the point of view character's personality and background? Are the words you use to describe the setting and other characters words your POV character would use? Do you mention any details that your POV character wouldn't be noticing in this scene? If yes, take them out.

9. Danger area 3 —
How to describe emotions

Readers read for the emotional experience. Without emotions, your book would be flat. Especially in character-driven stories such as romance novels, showing emotions instead of telling them is essential.

AVOID NAMING EMOTIONS

I mentioned before that you shouldn't name emotions because that is telling. I suggest that you create a list of emotion words that you often find yourself using. Use that list during the revision stage of every manuscript you write and use the find feature of your word processor to find these emotion words. Make sure you search for the noun, adjective, and adverb version of each word, e.g., anger, angry, angrily.

Sometimes, you can just cut out the emotion words because you have already shown what the character is feeling and the sentence works just fine without the *telling* addition.

Examples:

Showing and telling: She clapped her hands in delight.
Showing: She clapped her hands.

Showing and telling: `Tina's eyes narrowed angrily.`
Showing: `Tina's eyes narrowed.`

Showing and telling: `Frustrated, Tina threw up her hands.`
Showing: `Tina threw up her hands.`

EMOTION AS THE SUBJECT OF A SENTENCE

As I said in chapter 4, you don't have to cut out all emotion words. Sometimes, when you use an emotion as the subject of a sentence and pair it with a strong verb, it can work—but only if you use this technique sparingly.

Example:

`Relief flooded Tina's chest, making it hard for her to breathe.`

Of course, you could also show her relief without actually using the word.

Rewrite:

`Oh, thank God!` `She pressed her hand to her chest, trying to catch her breath.`

Most often, emotion words in your manuscript are a good indication that you will need to rewrite. There are better ways to reveal what your characters are feeling.

So, how do you do that?

EIGHT WAYS TO REVEAL EMOTION WITHOUT TELLING

Here are eight ways to reveal what your character is feeling:

1) Physical responses

Emotions always trigger physical responses. When we are afraid, our hearts start racing, our palms become sweaty, and our muscles tense. These are involuntary, visceral reactions that we have no control over. Make sure you describe physical sensations only for the POV character. If it's a non-POV character experiencing a certain emotion, we can only see the outward physical responses, for example, trembling hands.

Examples:

Telling: I was afraid.
Showing: Tremors wracked my body, and cold sweat trickled down my back.

Telling: She was angry.
Showing: Veins throbbed in her temples.

2) Body language and actions

Body language is a great way to show what a character feels. Remember to use strong, dynamic verbs to convey the emotion.

You might want to carry a notebook with you wherever you go so you can jot down the actions and body language that you observe in your everyday life. For example, I recently saw a pedestrian at a red traffic light bounce up and down on the balls of his feet—a great way to describe impatience.

Examples:

Telling: Betty was elated.

Showing: Betty twirled, her arms spread wide as if to hug the entire world.

Telling: She was ashamed of her knobby knees.

Showing: She lowered her lashes and tugged her skirt over her knobby knees.

Telling: I looked at Betty with annoyance.

Showing: I glared at Betty.

3) Facial expressions

Facial expressions are another wonderful way to convey emotions, but remember that you can only use them for non-POV characters. The POV character can't see her own face, so you can't describe what it looks like from the outside.

Try not to repeat the same facial expressions too often. In some manuscripts I edit, the characters—*all* characters—raise their eyebrows when they're surprised. Try to think of alternative, fresh ways to convey the emotion. *The Emotion Thesaurus: A Writer's Guide to Character Expression* by Angela Ackerman and Becca Puglisi can be a good start to thinking beyond the obvious.

Examples:

Telling: She was amused.

Showing: Her lips curled up in a smile.

Telling: She looked puzzled.

Showing: Her brow furrowed, and her eyes rolled upward as if seeking answers from above.

4) Dialogue

Make sure you use dialogue to reveal what your characters are feeling. It's a strong tool, since dialogue can—literally—speak for itself. If your characters are tense or angry, let them speak in shorter sentences and use words with harder sounds. If they are playful or in a reflective mood, make their sentences and words longer. And if your characters are nervous, they could stutter.

Examples:

Telling: I was so angry at John.
Showing: I smashed my fist onto the desk. "Goddammit, John!"

Telling: She waited impatiently.
Showing: She tapped her foot. "Come on. I'm not getting any younger here."

When writing dialogue, also don't forget to describe how your characters sound every now and then, but please don't resort to using adverbs and adjectives to do that.

Example:

Telling: "Space?" her mother repeated dejectedly. "From...from me?"
Showing: "Space?" Her mother sounded as if she'd slapped her. "From...from me?"

5) Internal monologue (thoughts)

Showing doesn't mean that you can only write about external things such as actions and dialogue. You can—and should—also dive into your character's mind. Internal monologue—or introspection—is another word for character thoughts. You can either present thoughts as direct internal monologue, written in first person and present tense and often set off by italics, or as indirect internal monologue in third person and past tense. Similar to when you're writing dialogue, the character's word choice can reveal his or her feelings.

Examples:

Telling: She was confused.
Showing (indirect internal monologue): What the hell was going on?

Telling: She tried hard to hide how jealous she was of her brother.
Showing (direct internal monologue): She struggled to keep her face expressionless as her father patted Tom's shoulder. *Yeah, of course, Daddy's golden child can do no wrong.*

6) Setting descriptions

The words you choose to describe a setting from a character's point of view can reveal a lot about what kind of mood he or she is in. The same setting can be seen in a different light, depending on what mood the POV character is in.

The weather or another part of the external setting can also mirror what your character is feeling.

Examples:

Telling: It rained heavily.
Showing (revealing an upbeat mood): Raindrops danced along the windowpane.
Showing (revealing a pessimistic mood): Rain lashed against the window.

7) The five senses

In moments of heightened emotion, our senses can also become heightened, so we're suddenly hyperaware of sounds or smells, for example.

Examples:

Telling: Afraid of whoever was following me, I walked faster.
Showing: Footsteps echoed behind me, and the stench of stale beer hit my nose. I walked faster.

8) Figurative language

Metaphors, similes, and other imagery can also be an effective way to reveal character emotions.

Examples:

Telling: She stared at him aggressively.
Showing: She stared at him like a prizefighter sizing up an opponent.

Just don't overdo it. If you have a simile or a metaphor in every paragraph, they will lose their power—especially if you use conflicting images, comparing your character with a prizefighter on one page, then with a ballerina on the next.

MAKE THE OUTWARD SIGNS OF EMOTIONS UNIQUE

Now that you know the eight methods you can use to show what your characters are feeling, remember that every character will reveal the same emotion in a different way. Some might start shouting and cursing when they are angry. Others get very quiet, with just a slight tightening of their lips giving them away. Some characters might not reveal any outward sign of emotion, so you'll need to show them through their thoughts.

So showing the way a character reveals emotions actually helps with characterization and gives us a better idea of who this character is deep inside. It shows so much more than just what he or she is feeling right now.

COMBINE EMOTION MARKERS TO AVOID AMBIGUITY

Sometimes, body language can be ambiguous and leave your readers not quite sure which emotions you are trying to portray. One action or facial expression doesn't always clearly identify the emotion.

Example:

    She scratched at the label of her beer bottle.

The character could be either bored or nervous. Maybe she's even angry at someone and taking it out on the beer bottle. You would have to add another piece of body language, dialogue, or internal monologue to make it clear which emotion she's feeling.

Example:

She scratched at the label of her beer bottle.
Where the heck was Toby? If he didn't show up
within the next five minutes, she'd be out of
here.

EXERCISE #9:

• Do another read-through of your chapter one. Are you naming any emotions and telling your readers what your characters are feeling? If so, rewrite and show your characters' emotions by using physical responses, body language, facial expressions, actions, dialogue, and internal monologue.

EXERCISE #10:

* Watch a movie or an episode of a TV show of your choice. Take notes on how the actors reveal emotions.

10. Telling in dialogue — How to recognize and fix it

I know I said that dialogue is a great way to show. But if you aren't careful, even dialogue can fall victim to telling.

Here's what you should keep an eye on to avoid telling when it comes to dialogue:

1) Maid-and-butler dialogue

Maid-and-butler dialogue, also called "as you know, Bob" dialogue, is a form of info-dumping through dialogue. The author wants to reveal some information to the reader, so he or she has the characters tell each other about that information, even though they both know about it already and have no reason to talk about it.

The term "maid-and-butler dialogue" is derived from theater. In the past, playwrights often had theater audiences "overhear" the butler and maid talk about the things the author wanted the audience to know. For example: "As you know, Bob, the master is away on business in London with his oldest son..."

Example:

"That's not a good idea," Betty said. "Remember what happened last time we tried that?"

"Remind me again?" Tina said.

"Well, our freshman year in college, when we lived with that guy whose girlfriend stayed over all the time..."

"Roy."

"Yes, I know."

In real life, all Betty would say is probably: "That's not a good idea. Remember what happened when we tried that on Roy's girlfriend?"

In many places, the maid-and-butler dialogue can simply be cut. Readers don't need to know all the information, at least not right away. If it's information that readers really need, find a more natural way to let them know. Having a character present who doesn't know the information yet and asks about it is sometimes an option. Give your characters a good reason to talk about it.

2) "Creative" dialogue tags

Some authors seem to think that readers will get bored with *said* as a dialogue tag, so they try to come up with more creative dialogue tags such as *exclaimed, demanded,* or *commented.*

Normally, variety and creativity are good things when you're a writer, but this is an exception. The best dialogue tag is always *said* because it's unobtrusive and doesn't distract from the dialogue itself.

If you use dialogue tags other than said (or maybe asked and answered), you're telling. Avoid dialogue tags that explain the dialogue to your readers and let the dialogue speak for itself. If the line of dialogue itself doesn't tell readers how it is spoken, your dialogue is weak and needs to be revised.

Example:

Telling: "Can't keep up with me?" she teased.
Showing: "Can't keep up with me, old woman?"

Telling: "It wasn't him. It was me," I confessed.
Showing: "It wasn't him," I said. "It was me."

It the words themselves clearly are a confession, you don't need to tell your readers so in the dialogue tag, or they'll feel patronized.

3) Adverbs in dialogue tags

Using adverbs in dialogue tags is a form of telling too. The emotion should be visible in the dialogue itself, and it can also be revealed through body language and facial expressions, so you don't need the adverb.

Example:

Telling: "Isn't my garden beautiful?" she said smugly.
Showing: "That's one fine looking garden, isn't it?" She polished her nails on her shirt.

Telling: "Get out," I said angrily.
Showing: "Get out." I shoved him toward the door.

4) Reported dialogue

Reported dialogue—sometimes called indirect dialogue—is when you, the author, are *telling* your readers what one character said without *showing* the actual words in quotation marks. Most often, you should avoid reported dialogue since it's another form of telling.

Example:

Telling: Tina explained that she hadn't seen him in a while.

Showing: "I haven't seen him in a while," Tina said.

Telling: Tina asked how often they went to the zoo.

Showing: "How often do you go to the zoo?" Tina asked.

If the conversation is important, show it. And if it's not important because it doesn't move your plot forward, cut it. There are a few instances, however, where reported dialogue might actually be preferable. More about that in the chapter on the uses of telling.

EXERCISE #11:

• Read through the first chapter of your manuscript again. This time, look for any places where you might have slipped into telling when it comes to dialogue.

• Are your characters telling each other things they both already know? If yes, consider whether it's really necessary for readers to have this information now and if it is, find other ways to reveal this information to your readers.

• Are you using a lot of dialogue tags other than *said, answered*, and *asked*? Replace some of them with *said, answered*, or *asked*.

• Are you using adverbs in your dialogue tags? Cut most adverbs.

• Is there any reported dialogue in your first chapter? Consider rewriting and actually *showing* your readers the conversation, unless it really isn't important.

11. Overshowing —
How to avoid showing too much

After all the positive things I've said about showing, it might be hard
to believe, but there actually is such a thing as too much showing. If
you take the "show, don't tell" advice too far and show your readers
every little detail, even the unimportant ones, your story will get
bogged down.

OVERSHOWING ON A MACRO LEVEL

Don't overload your readers with long blocks of descriptions that
might not even be important. Too many details distract the reader
from the story and make your book drag. For every sentence
you write, ask yourself if your readers really need this piece of
information. Does it contribute to the scene's goal, reveal something
interesting about your character, or move the plot forward? If the
answers are no, leave out this piece of information.

Especially try to keep unimportant details out of your opening
chapter. Don't start your novel with mundane actions such as
your character waking up and getting ready to go to work—unless
something interesting happens to interrupt that routine.

Example:

> Leaving Jake staring after her in the kitchen, Tina walked toward the hallway and then made a left toward her bedroom. When she passed the bathroom, she stopped and went in to get her makeup case before continuing on to the bedroom.
>
> With the floor-to-ceiling window, the room had heated up even though it was barely ten. Would it be as hot in Chicago right now? She reminded herself to pack some sunscreen and a hat. She went to her wardrobe and pulled out three pair of jeans, two dresses, and several sweatshirts. She set them on a dresser before pulling out her drawers and taking out some underwear, which she added to the pile on the dresser.

Of all these details, which ones are important? Does your reader really need to know how many pairs of jeans she's packing? Do they need to know the layout of rooms and every step she takes to get from the kitchen to her bedroom?

What is and isn't important depends on where you are going with your story, of course. But a revised scene might look like this:

Example:

> Leaving Jake staring after her, she marched toward the bedroom and threw her suitcase onto her bed. Fuck Jake. She would be going to Chicago, with or without him.

Isn't that much more interesting than watching her go through every article in her wardrobe? And we're getting the same essential information as in the longer, more boring paragraphs above—she's packing to go to Chicago.

OVERSHOWING ON A MICRO LEVEL

Sometimes, overshowing isn't just happening on a macro level—paragraphs of information that we as readers don't really need—but also on the micro level of single actions and sentences.

Example:

```
She reached out her right hand, grabbed the
doorknob, turned it, and pushed the door open.
```

That's a lot of detail. For example, does it really matter whether she uses her right hand or the left one to open the door? Since your readers all know how to open a door, you don't need to give them that level of detail—unless you want to slow down the scene to increase the tension because there's a killer waiting on the other side of the door. But if the character is just entering her home after a day at work, this is too much showing.

Rewrite:

```
She opened the door.
```

Another example:

```
She opened her mouth and groaned.
```

If she groans, we can assume that she opened her mouth to do so.

Rewrite:

`She groaned.`

In general, showing is great, but don't go overboard or it will slow the pace of your story. Show what is important, and cut the rest.

EXERCISE #12:

- Look at your first chapter once more. Have you been showing too much? Are there any paragraphs of information that readers don't necessarily need or that aren't important to the plot? Take them out.

- Also take a look at the sentence level. Are single actions described using too much detail? Can you simplify?

12. The uses of telling — When telling is the better choice

Most often, "show, don't tell" is good advice, but telling isn't always bad. Sometimes, it's even preferable to showing.

So, when is it better to tell?

There are eight situations when telling might be the better choice:

1) Unimportant details

When you compare the telling examples with the ones that show, you probably realize that showing takes up more space on the page. The more space you give to something in your story, the more important it will seem. Showing is a signal to readers that what you're writing about is important, so they'd better pay attention. If you show everything, readers will assume everything is important and they'll eventually become exhausted. The really important things won't stand out anymore.

Thus, save the showing for the important parts that move the plot forward or reveal something about the characters and their emotional states. All of the crucial moments in your story, especially the climax, should be shown.

Telling uses fewer words than showing; it can be used to compress information that is not all that important but that you still want your readers to know. Use telling to sum up mundane or unimportant parts instead of wasting words on things that really aren't important. Often, these are everyday activities such as taking a shower, getting dressed, driving to work, or cooking dinner. You're writing a novel, not a cook book, so you don't need to provide a step-by-step description of your character preparing dinner—unless it's important to the plot, for example, she's adding poison to the spaghetti sauce.

Example:

Showing: I moved my mouse to the top-right corner of the screen and clicked on the X icon to close the browser.
Telling: I closed the browser.

Another example, this one from my short story "Seduction for Beginners":

They ordered, and within fifteen minutes the waiter returned with the fries and two Caesar salads.

Here, my two main characters are enjoying a romantic dinner, but I want the focus to be on their conversation, the emotions, not on their interaction with the waiter, so instead of showing the ordering process, I summed it up ("they ordered") and jumped ahead in time.

For more examples of unimportant details and how they can be summed up by *telling*, take a look at the previous chapter.

2) Transitions

Telling can be useful for transitions between scenes, when you are jumping ahead in time, switch point of view, or jump to another location. You can use telling to summarize a span of time or distance and debrief your readers on what happened in between the scenes.

Example:

> After three days without a call from John, Tina had enough.

You can use telling for transitions not just at the beginning, but at the end of a scene too. Telling helps to move your readers into or out of scenes.

Example:

> Betty locked her apartment door and went to work.

"Went to work" is telling. Unless something exciting, for example, an accident, happens on the way to work, you don't need to show the car ride. Sum it up by telling readers that she went to work.

3) Repeated information

Most of the time, you should avoid showing readers the same thing twice. Telling can be a great way to avoid repeating information. For example, it can be used to summarize when one character is telling another about something that the reader witnessed happening.

Example from my novel *Shaken to the Core*:

> "What's he doing?" Kate whispered and looked around. "Doesn't he know that the mayor banned the sale of alcohol? If the soldiers catch him, he'll have the wine poured out—or worse!"

> Giuliana didn't want an overeager soldier to
> shoot Luigi, so she hurried toward him and told
> him what Kate had just said.

The "told him what Kate had just said" is telling—but in this case, the good form of telling. Using reported dialogue saves me from having to repeat Kate's words.

4) Repeated events

You can also use telling to summarize events that happen repeatedly. For example, in my historical romance *Backwards to Oregon*, the main characters are traveling along the Oregon Trail in a wagon train. On their journey, they have to cross several rivers. If I showed it every time, it would quickly get repetitive and boring for readers, so I showed only one dramatic river crossing and summed up the rest.

Example:

> The Sweetwater was notorious for twisting back
> on itself. Unlike the river, the emigrants had
> somewhere to be and weren't content to meander
> across the landscape, so they were forced to
> cross the river time after time.

5) Pacing

If you show too much, it can slow down the pace of your story. If you show every little thing, you will end up with a dragging 500,000-word novel. So whenever showing would disrupt the forward momentum of your story, you can tell instead. Telling is great if you need to deliver a piece of information to the reader quickly, without slowing down the pace. For example, sometimes it's better to just say "he smiled" instead of "his lips quirked up, and his crow's feet deepened."

Telling can also give your readers a bit of a breather after the nonstop action of the previous scenes.

6) Context

A little bit of telling right before a scene can provide context. For example, it can sum up the slow development that culminates in this scene, or it can set up a routine that is interrupted by something out of the ordinary that is now happening.

You can also use telling to sum up slow, steady developments. Of course, you will still have to show the critical moments in that development in dramatized scenes, but telling can give an impression of the things happening in between these moments.

Example from *Heartwood* by Catherine Lane:

> Their afternoons were pretty much written in stone. After lunch, they took their customary walk in the woods so Dawn could say hello to her favorite tree. Every day, she would bury her face in its trunk and whisper secrets into the dark red bark.
>
> "What're you telling it?" Beth had finally asked on one walk.

The first paragraph is telling. It's not written in real time but sums up how they spend their afternoons. The second paragraph—the line of dialogue—starts the action in real time for which the first paragraph provided the context.

7) Suspense

You can also use telling to create suspense by arousing an expectation in your readers.

Example:

> Tina hated first days. Her first day of kindergarten, she had hid in her mother's closet. First day of elementary school, she'd been sick all over the teacher. It hadn't helped that her family had moved all over the country, so she'd gone through eight first days in a new town, at a new school, where the teacher would inevitably get her name wrong.
>
> Today, her first day at Kudos Entertainment Inc., would be different, though.

Telling readers about all the first days gone wrong, they will start to wonder what will go wrong on her first day at the new job.

8) First drafts

Another place where telling is just fine is the first draft of your story. Don't feel as if you have to get all the showing right in the first draft. As James Thurber once said: *Don't get it right; just get it written.* During the first-draft stage, focus on the big picture—the plot and the characters. If trying to show would slow you down too much, go ahead and tell. During the revision stage, go back over your entire manuscript and check for places where you need to turn telling into showing. Many writers find it easier to get the story down first and worry about turning it into vivid prose later.

FIND THE RIGHT BALANCE

So, as you can see, telling definitely has its uses. Maybe the best advice to give to writers isn't to "show, don't tell," but to "show and tell." A good story requires both, so writers need both showing and telling skills in their writing toolboxes. The trick is to strike the right balance and figure out when it's better to show (which is most of the time) and when it's better to tell.

Use showing and telling deliberately and combine them to create just the right effect. Make your scenes come to life by showing your characters in action and showing their emotions and support these dramatized scenes with telling that compresses time and sums up unimportant information quickly.

THREE OPTIONS

To sum it up, for every piece of information you gave your readers in your first draft, consider three options during the revisions:

- **Show it** — If it's important, show it. That's always true for your characters' emotions.
- **Tell it** — If it's less important but still needed, tell it. For example, readers might need to know that two weeks have gone by, but they don't need to see every minute of these two weeks, so use telling as a transition.
- **Leave it out** — If it's not important to the plot, consider leaving it out.

MAKE YOUR TELLING WORK

Since I advised you to *show, don't tell* for most of this book, you might think that telling is bad writing. As I just said, telling has its uses, and you can write your telling passages in a way that doesn't make your readers want to skip them. Here's how to make your telling more effective:

- Make sure it's a piece of information that readers really need to have.
- Avoid repetition. Never tell something that you have already shown.
- Keep it short.
- Use strong, vivid verbs and concrete nouns.
- Make it interesting! Readers won't even notice that you're telling if a sentence or a paragraph grabs their attention.

Example from my novel *Damage Control*:

```
Nick's frown deepened the little scar on his
forehead. He liked to tell people that it was
from one of the stunts in his movies, when he'd
actually tripped in the bathroom and hit his
head on the toilet.
```

The first sentence shows Nick's emotion. The second sentence is telling readers a bit of backstory, but my beta readers told me they found it interesting anyway.

EXERCISE #13:

- Take one last look at your chapter one, or—if you feel up to it—look at the first five chapters. Are there any places where telling would be better?
- Take a look at the very beginnings of your chapters and scenes. Could you use telling to provide some information on how much time has passed or where the new chapter is taking place?
- Could you use telling to create context for the scene that is about to begin?
- Look at your chapter endings and beginnings. Could you use telling to create suspense?
- Could you use telling to avoid repeating information or to sum up unimportant information?

EXERCISE #14:

• Get some highlighters (red and blue) and an inexpensive paperback copy of your favorite novel. Make sure it's a novel in the same genre as your own and one that has been published within the last five years. While I value the classics, the writing techniques that worked in the past are no longer working for modern readers.

• Take a look at the opening scene. Highlight every line of showing in blue and every line of telling in red. Do this again for the climax of the story—the scene in which the central conflict of the story is resolved. Look at the balance of showing vs. telling. Usually, the climax should have less telling than the opening because the opening sets up the story while the climactic scene should show the protagonist overcoming a major obstacle or have an important realization or a moment of change.

• Now do the same with your opening scene and your climax. How does it compare?

EXERCISE #15:

- Give your manuscript to at least one beta reader—an avid reader or a fellow writer who will read your manuscript and provide you with feedback. Ask your beta readers to flag all parts of the story were they are getting bored or feel their attention drifting.
- Take a look at the parts that your beta reader flagged. Chances are, your beta reader got bored because you either told too much—in which case you should rewrite and *show*—or because you showed too much—in which case you should cut unimportant details or, if they are somewhat important, sum them up with telling, as demonstrated in this chapter and the previous chapter.

13. Exercises —
How to exercise your showing skills

Now that you know how to recognize telling and how to show, let's practice what you just learned.

Get out a notebook, a laptop, a piece of paper, or your preferred choice of writing material. Below, you will find twenty examples of telling. After every example, stop reading and write down a possible revision that turns telling into showing.

Once you wrote down your solution, you can compare it to my suggestion in chapter 14.

1. She was cold.
2. It was hot outside.
3. He looked tired.
4. She was overweight.
5. The house was run-down.
6. It was a dark and stormy night.
7. She seemed uncomfortable.
8. I felt relieved.
9. He was helpless.
10. It was raining as she drove.
11. I ate dinner.

12. The pizza looked delicious, but it tasted horrible.
13. I was jealous of my neighbor's new car.
14. She was afraid.
15. She was curious.
16. Tina was a spoiled child.
17. When her brother refused to give her the book, she became angry.
18. Satisfied that everything was packed, Tina grabbed her bag.
19. The view over the entire city was soothing.
20. The cabin was romantic.

Once you wrote down your solutions, you can compare them to my suggestions in chapter 14.

DOWNLOAD MORE WRITING EXERCISES

Or, if you're in the mood for more writing exercises, pay a visit to my website, where you can find more exercises and solutions that will help you improve your showing skills. You can download them for free at: http:/sandragerth.com/exercises-showing

14. Solutions —
How to rewrite the telling in
chapter 13

If you sat down and took the time to try the exercises in chapter 13, you should now have a list of thirteen sentences or paragraphs that *show*.

Now you can compare your solutions with mine. Keep in mind that there is no right or wrong answer for these exercises. The solutions I came up with are only meant to give you an idea of how showing could work; other writers will come up with solutions that are different but just as good. The possibilities are endless.

1. Telling: She was cold.
    Showing: Her teeth chattered as she blew on her fingers.

2. Telling: It was hot outside.
    Showing: Heat sizzled from the pavement. She wiped her sweaty brow and tried not to gag at the stench of rotting garbage on the sidewalks.

3. Telling: He looked tired.
    Showing: He slumped into his chair. His eyelids drooped, and his chin sank on his chest.

4. Telling: She was overweight.
   Showing: As she heaved herself up from her chair, Jake halfway expected to hear a groan of relief from the piece of furniture.

5. Telling: The house was run-down.
   Showing: Paint flaked from the walls. Weeds had taken over the cracks in the driveway. The smell of mildew, mold, and urine filled Tina's nostrils as she stepped over broken glass.

6. Telling: It was a dark and stormy night.
   Showing: The wind rattled the shutters and hurled rain from the night sky.

7. Telling: She seemed uncomfortable.
   Showing: She slid to the edge of her seat and shuffled her feet beneath the table.

8. Telling: I felt relieved.
   Showing: The tension in my shoulders eased.

9. Telling: He was helpless.
   Showing: He rubbed his temples. What was he supposed to do now?

10. Telling: It was raining as she drove.
    Showing: Rain drummed on the windshield and the Honda's roof, drowning out the hum of the engine.

11. Telling: I ate dinner.
    Showing: I cut into her juicy steak. The scent of herb butter teased my nose.

12. **Telling:** The pizza looked delicious, but it tasted horrible.

    Showing: Steam rising up off the melted cheese made his mouth water. He picked up a slice and took a huge bite. A bitter taste spread across his tongue. *Ugh. Dammit.* Who the hell had put olives on his pizza?

13. **Telling:** I was jealous of my neighbor's new car.

    Showing: I trailed my fingertips over the gleaming hood of John's jaguar. It was warm and sleek to the touch. My other hand clenched around my keys, the hard edges digging into my fingers as I wrestled down the urge to scratch the polished surface.

14. **Telling:** She was afraid.

    Showing: She wrapped her arms around herself and wiped her palms, wet with perspiration, on the back of her shirt.

15. **Telling:** She was curious.

    Showing: She tilted her head to the side and waved her hand in a gimme motion. "Come on. Tell me!"

16. **Telling:** Tina was a spoiled child.

    Showing: Tina threw herself on the floor and flailed her arms and legs. "I want it! I want it! I want it!"

17. **Telling:** When her brother refused to give her the book, she became angry.
Showing: Blood roared in her ears. She thrust her chin forward. "If you don't give me that damn book back, I'll kill you."

18. **Telling:** Satisfied that everything was packed, Tina grabbed her bag.
Showing: Great. Everything was packed. Tina grabbed her bag.

19. **Telling:** The view over the entire city was soothing.
Showing: Tina gripped the balustrade. A grid of lights stretched out as far as she could see, and the miniature shapes of skyscrapers in the distance reminded her that life went on for millions of people. It would go on for her too. Her death grip on the balustrade eased.

20. **Telling:** The cabin was romantic.
Showing: The flames in the wood-burning fireplace crackled. The moon shone down on them through the skylight in the cross-beam ceiling.

15. Conclusion — What to do now

In this book, you learned a lot about how to recognize telling and how to turn telling passages into scenes that *show*.

If you read each chapter and completed the exercises at the end of each, you should now have a fairly good idea of how to *show*. In addition, you should have a first chapter that draws your readers into your story.

But that's really just the beginning. Every newly acquired skill has to be practiced. The best advice won't do you any good if you don't incorporate it into your writing. So once you have completed revising the first chapter of your novel, continue with the rest of the manuscript, using the techniques discussed in this book.

Keep revising until you are happy with each scene, and keep coming back to this book for pointers and refreshers.

You might also want to keep an eye on how other writers employ these tools. Whenever you read a book, be aware of what pulls you in as a reader so that you can use these techniques in your own writing.

Thank you for taking the time to read this book. I hope you found it helpful. If you did, I would appreciate it if you would leave a review where you bought it. That might help other writers understand the powerful principle of show, don't tell and improve their writing skills too.

Thank you for your support!

About Sandra Gerth

Sandra Gerth is a writer and an editor who divides her time between writing her own books and helping other writers revise and polish theirs.

She holds a degree in psychology and worked as a psychologist for eight years before transitioning into a career as a full-time novelist—the best job in the world as far as she's concerned.

She earned a certificate in editing from the Academy of German Book Trade and is now the senior editor of Ylva Publishing, a small press that publishes women's fiction.

Under her pen name, Jae, she has published fourteen novels and about two dozen short stories. Her books have won numerous awards and have been #1 best-sellers on Amazon on various occasions.

She's also the author of a series of books for writers.

CONNECT WITH SANDRA GERTH:

Website: www.sandragerth.com

Other books from
Ylva Publishing

www.ylva-publishing.com

Goal Setting for Writers

(Writers' Guide Series)

How to set and achieve your writing goals, finally write a book, and become a successful author

Sandra Gerth

ISBN: 978-3-95533-358-4 (mobi), 978-3-95533-359-1 (epub)
Length: 39,000 words

Writing a book is on the bucket list of millions of people worldwide, but very few actually finish their book or manage to fulfill other writing dreams such as making a living as a writer.

Many writers fail because they don't know how to set effective writing goals and how to develop an action plan that will turn their dreams into reality.

Whether you are a complete newbie just thinking about writing your first book or a multi-published author dreaming of becoming a full-time writer or somewhere in between, this book will help you to:

- Learn the difference between dreams and goals,
- Turn your dreams into effective, realistic writing goals,
- Discover what matters most to you about your writing,
- Break down your goals into bite-sized chunks that you can achieve more easily, even if you don't have much time to write,
- Create an action plan that guides you through every step of the writing and publishing process, from brainstorming ideas to marketing,
- Overcome procrastination, writer's block, and other obstacles that keep you from finishing your book.

Time Management for Writers

(Writers' Guide Series)

How to write faster, find the time to write your book, and be a more prolific writer

Sandra Gerth

ISBN: 978-3-95533-553-3 (mobi), 978-3-95533-554-0 (epub)
Length: 45,000 words

In the digital age, publishing as book is easier than ever, but finding the time to write a book is becoming harder and harder. With day jobs, family obligations, household chores, and hobbies, many writers struggle to get any writing done. At the same time, publishers and readers expect writers to publish multiple books every year and to somehow find enough time to market their books through blogging, social media, and networking. If you are struggling to find enough time to write or don't get much written once you finally do, this book is for you. Whether you write fiction or nonfiction, this book will help you to

- Find enough time to write, even if you have a day job,
- Write and publish more books in less time,
- Use rituals to create a powerful writing habit,
- Get your first drafts written more quickly, while still writing well,
- Deal with distractions and interruptions,
- Find your most productive writing routine and environment,
- Use writing challenges to become more productive,
- Discover tools and resources that help you focus on your writing,
- Manage your e-mail inbox in less time,
- Decide how much time to spend writing versus marketing,
- Overcome writer's block and procrastination.

Point of View

(Writers' Guide Series)

How to use the different POV types, avoid head-hopping, and choose the best point of view for your book

Sandra Gerth

ISBN: 978-3-95533-751-3 (mobi), 978-3-95533-752-0 (epub)

Length: 23,000 words

Point of view (POV) is one of the most powerful tools in a writer's kit, but it's also one of the hardest to understand and master.

In this book, Sandra Gerth draws on her experience as an editor and a best-selling author to teach you how to handle point of view in a way that will make your readers identify with your main character, draw them into the story, and keep them captivated until the very last page. Whether you're a novice writer working on her first story or an established author, this book will help you to:

- Discover what point of view is and why it's so important.
- Understand the different types of point of view such as first-person, third-person, omniscient, and deep POV.
- Choose the point of view that works best for your story.
- Write a novel from multiple viewpoints without confusing your readers.
- Avoid head-hopping and other POV violations that would throw your readers out of the story.
- Write internal monologue and take your readers deeply into your character's mind.
- Create suspense and tension by using POV techniques.
- Let your readers experience events through your main character's eyes to get them emotionally involved in your story.

Show, Don't Tell. How to write vivid descriptions, handle backstory, and describe your characters' emotions.
© by Sandra Gerth

ISBN: 978-3-95533-750-6

Also available as e-book.

Published by Ylva Publishing, legal entity of Ylva Verlag, e.Kfr.
Ylva Verlag, e.Kfr.
Owner: Astrid Ohletz
Am Kirschgarten 2
65830 Kriftel
Germany

www.ylva-publishing.com

First edition: 2016

Credits
Cover Concept Art by Streetlight Graphics

Made in the USA
Middletown, DE
01 May 2019